Paragraph Writing Made Easy!

by
Rosemary Shiras
and
Susan Cary Smith

SCHOLASTIC
PROFESSIONAL BOOKS

NEW YORK • TORONTO • LONDON • AUCKLAND • SYDNEY
MEXICO CITY • NEW DELHI • HONG KONG • BUENOS AIRES

Acknowledgments

We are indebted to the following people for their invaluable assistance:

Peter Shiras

Susan Vodrey

Nancy Hall

Liza Ketchum

Sally L. Smith

Trudie Lamb Richmond

Arthur Rosenblatt

Jean Bronson

Sandra Crehore

Patricia Snodgrass

Fenn School Students

Cover design by Josué Castilleja
Cover illustration by Mike Moran
Interior design by Solutions by Design, Inc.
Interior illustrations by Kate Flanagan

ISBN 0-439-20764-9

Table of Contents

Why We Wrote This Book—A Personal Letter to Teachers
by Rosemary Shiras

"We shall all wait quietly while Rosemary tries to answer the question about the paragraph we have just read."

I was 13 years old. I had read the paragraph in Twain's *Huckleberry Finn,* and there were parts I didn't understand. There were always parts I didn't understand. But I never reread those parts; I never asked questions. Instead I slumped in my seat, hoping I wouldn't be called on. When the teacher said, "Rosemary," I was frozen with fright and embarrassment, unable to respond. No one had taught me the essential skill of understanding paragraphs. This incident is etched in my memory. I was afraid to take risks and ask questions.

When I began teaching, I discovered that many of my students weren't confident learners either. Students in English, social studies, and science classes were asked to write reports without having been taught the necessary preliminary writing skills. After seeing my students stumble again and again, unable to express themselves clearly in writing, I decided to write lessons that would give them the writing skills they'd need throughout school and later in life. Understanding and writing paragraphs—a very basic yet often neglected skill—is the focus of this book.

After working for five years on the text, I joined forces with Susan Smith. She revised and wrote instructions, organized the sequence of the text, added new material, piloted the program in her classroom, and arranged for teachers to use and critique the lessons. The techniques in this book were used at her middle school for four years. During this time, we've seen students demonstrate significant improvement in comprehension and writing. Perhaps most gratifying has been their growing confidence as learners and their enthusiastic reactions to their successes. As one student commented, "I love this work!"

Introduction

Paragraph Writing Made Easy! teaches students how to organize information and use it to express ideas coherently. These basic skills prepare students to write paragraphs, essays, and reports. This book's tight focus on analyzing and writing paragraphs enables students to gain a solid foundation for their future writing.

The lessons and student exercises in Understanding Paragraphs, Section 1 of the book, teach students how to read and understand various types of paragraphs, and then take notes on them in outline form. The lessons and exercises in Writing Paragraphs, Section 2, teach students how to use their notes to write their own well-constructed paragraphs. The ability to use an outline, the first step in the writing process, provides students with an organized structure that enables them to make a plan, think and talk about the plan, and then write. The writing exercises in Section 2 reinforce all the skills students have already learned and are structured so that students become more and more independent and confident as they convert the Practice Outlines into paragraphs.

Each lesson begins with a Teacher Page that explains objectives and procedures. Student Pages that follow introduce or review a skill. Each group of Student Pages begins with an introduction and sample paragraphs for you to use to introduce and discuss the skill so that students know exactly what they'll be expected to learn. Use the examples as a springboard for questions, clarification, and discussion. Following these introductory materials, there are a series of Practice Paragraphs or Outlines for students to work on independently. Students keep the Student Pages in their own notebooks for review. After students have completed all the exercises, each student will have a 58-page personal paragraph handbook to refer to again and again as he or she writes.

You may find you need to spend two or three class periods on each concept or specific skill introduced. Keep the pace slow. Allow plenty of time for questions and discussion. It's important for you to help your students develop the habit of thinking about the topic before they practice on their own. For example, what do they already know about the topic? How can they use this information as they read? When your students have finished writing a paragraph, ask them to evaluate what they've written to be sure they've communicated what they were trying to say. This review helps them realize that writing is a step-by-step process that requires writing, revising and rewriting, and proofreading. As students begin to understand how paragraphs work and see their skills improving with practice and repetition, you'll find fewer explanations are needed.

The suggested answers on pages 74–81 provide sample answers and can serve as a quick check for you.

LESSON 1
Paragraph Construction

Purpose

The purpose of this lesson is to introduce students to the concept of the paragraph and how it is constructed.

Materials Needed

- set of three-hole-punched copies of Lesson 1 Student Pages (pages 7–12) for each student
- three-ring binder for each student

Suggested Procedure

Distribute a set of Student Pages to each student. The student lesson is organized so that the first pages present students with new material and the following pages provide practice and reinforcement. With students, go over the pages that introduce new information and examples to make sure they understand the skills being taught. You may want to choose some of the Practice Paragraphs for students to do on their own for additional practice with a particular skill. This practice may entail providing background information about the topic, introducing new vocabulary, and giving more practice with a particular skill. Have students store the Student Pages in their binders.

Follow-Up

Students can use the completed activities in their binders as a resource for future reference.

Reinforce the skills—identifying a topic, key words, topic sentence, supporting sentences—introduced in this lesson when students are reading other materials.

Concepts to Be Taught

- paragraph
- topic
- key words
- topic sentence
- supporting sentences

Skills to Be Learned

Students will be able to identify the topic (using key words), the topic sentence, and supporting sentences in a paragraph.

Name _____ Date _____

Paragraph Construction

To be a good writer, you have to understand how paragraphs are constructed. A single paragraph is a group of sentences that has one central idea or *topic*. Usually, one of the sentences presents the topic to be discussed. This sentence is called the *topic sentence*. The topic sentence is the *focus* of the paragraph. All of the other sentences in the paragraph support, or explain, the idea expressed in the topic sentence. These are called *supporting sentences*.

Example 1: **Read the following paragraph.**

> Birds are animals with distinctive characteristics. For example, all birds have feathers. Birds also have beaks rather than teeth and wings instead of arms. In addition, birds lay eggs.

The central idea, or topic, in this paragraph is *birds,* and the topic sentence is: *Birds are animals with distinctive characteristics.* It tells what the paragraph is about. The other sentences in the paragraph are supporting sentences. They support, give further meaning to, and provide details about the topic sentence by explaining the characteristics of birds:

- all birds have feathers
- birds have beaks rather than teeth
- birds have wings instead of arms
- birds lay eggs

Example 2: **Here is another example of a paragraph. It has a topic, a topic sentence, and supporting sentences that give details about the topic.**

topic → sentence

Foods full of sugar are high in calories and can be bad for your health. For example, one pound of candy has about 250 grams of sugar and one pound of apples has 48 grams of sugar. A 12-ounce can of cola has about 9 teaspoonfuls of sugar and a 12-ounce → detail sentences grape juice drink has about 2 teaspoonfuls. Too much sugar often results in tooth cavities, hyperactivity, fatigue, and obesity.

Name _____ Date _____

Example 3: In order to identify the topic of a paragraph, you may find a word or words that are repeated. These words are called *key words*. Key words give you a clue about the topic. Read the following paragraph carefully and look for a key word.

What is blood? Blood contains red blood cells that carry oxygen and nutrients to various parts of the body. Blood also contains white blood cells that help fight disease. Blood contains disklike platelets that assist in clotting.

The key word is *blood,* and it is repeated six times. The topic of this paragraph is blood.

Example 4: Read the following paragraph. Circle the key words. What is the topic of the paragraph?

Cargo ships carry goods from one port to another. One kind of cargo ship is a container ship, which carries goods in large crates called containers. Another kind of cargo ship carries bulk food such as grains, which are poured down chutes into the ship's hold. A third kind of cargo ship carries trucks and trains, which can be driven on and off the ship.

The key words are *cargo ship* and they are repeated four times. The topic of this paragraph is cargo ships.

Paragraph Writing Made Easy! Scholastic Professional Books

Name _____ Date _____

Example 5: After you find the key words which help you identify the topic, you need to find topic sentence, the one sentence that presents the topic to be discussed. Read the following paragraph carefully. Find the key word and circle it each time it is used. What is the topic? See if you can find the topic sentence.

> Spiders trap food in various ways. Some spiders make webs. Other spiders use a thread of silk like a lasso. Still other spiders live in the ground and come out to hunt. A few spiders live in flowers and camouflage themselves. Others live underwater and hunt at night.

The key word is *spiders,* and it is repeated five times. The topic of this paragraph is spiders. However, notice that the whole paragraph is not about spiders in general. It has a specific focus. Look at the first sentence in the paragraph. This sentence tells you the focus of the paragraph: *how spiders trap food.* The first sentence, *Spiders trap food in various ways,* is the topic sentence. This sentence is supported by five detail sentences that give examples of how spiders trap food.

Example 6: Read the following paragraph. Find and underline the topic sentence. It will help if you first find the repeated key word (or words)—the words that give you a clue about the topic.

> The eagle has a strong, hooked beak to catch live animals. The avocet, a shorebird, has a long beak to go deep into the mud to get shellfish. Woodpeckers have strong beaks to hammer holes into trees to find insects under the bark. The tropical toucans have enormous beaks and reach into fruit trees to find nuts and fruit. Over time, birds' beaks have adapted to the way they find their food.

The key words, *beak* and *beaks,* are repeated five times. The topic is birds' beaks. Notice that the whole paragraph is not about birds' beaks in general but has a specific focus. The specific focus is that birds' beaks have various shapes that enable them to find food. The topic sentence is at the end of the paragraph: *Nature has made birds' beaks adapt to the way they find their food.* The rest of the sentences are examples that support this sentence.

More About Topic Sentences

Topic sentences can come in different places in a paragraph. Often the topic sentence will be at the beginning of a paragraph. However, in some paragraphs the topic sentence is in the middle or at the end of the paragraph.

Name _____ Date _____

Practice Paragraphs

Read the following paragraphs. Circle the key words in each one. Find and underline the topic sentence.

1. During the Vietnam War about 55,000 nurses cared for 300,000 wounded soldiers. The nurses cared for soldiers maimed by land mines, injured by gunfire, or ill with diseases. In addition, the nurses comforted those who were in great mental and physical pain. The nurses' jobs were never-ending.

Key Word: _____ Number of Times It Appears: _____

2. The number of courses served in a railroad dining car in the 1920s made dinner a memorable event. The first course was soup, such as yellow pea soup or crab bisque. The second course was a fish, such as poached salmon or Chesapeake flounder. The next course of the meal was the main meat course, perhaps venison or sugar-cured ham. Side orders of vegetables might include rice fritters, baked tomatoes, spinach Florentine, or potatoes Romanoff. Salad was the next course. Diners could choose between fresh fruit salad or endive and watercress salad. Delicious desserts, the final course, included rhubarb and strawberry cake, chocolate mousse, or brandy flip pie. Coffee or tea concluded the meal.

Key Word: _____ Number of Times It Appears: _____

Paragraph Writing Made Easy! Scholastic Professional Books

Name _____ Date _____

Read the following paragraphs. Circle the key word each time it appears. You should know that a pronoun that refers to a key word is also considered a key word. Find and underline the topic sentence.

3.   A palindrome is a word or a sentence that is spelled the same backward as forward. Some word palindromes are pep, noon, Anna, and madam. A palindrome sentence is Step on no pets. It is fun to think of palindromes. Can you think of others?

   Key Word: _____   **Number of Times It Appears:** _____

4.   Jackie Robinson was one of the cleverest base runners in modern baseball. He made the pitcher nervous by dancing back and forth on the base path. He broke the pitcher's concentration. Then he went from standing still to full speed in one step. When Jackie Robinson was at third base, he usually scored. In 1949 he stole 37 bases, the most of any National League player between 1930 and 1956.

   Key Word: _____   **Number of Times It Appears:** _____

5.   From the time the artist Georgia O'Keeffe was young, she was interested in painting a part of a whole scene. For example, when studying the orchid, she would focus on one part of the flower, such as the stamen. When looking at a sunflower, she chose petals as the part she wished to paint. Even in the desert, she would focus on the shape of a buffalo skull. Often she chose to concentrate only on the door of a building rather than the whole building. Georgia O'Keeffe would look at a whole scene, and then choose one part of the scene to become her primary focus.

   Key Word: _____   **Number of Times It Appears:** _____

Name _____ Date _____

6.   In 1955 Claudette Colvin, a 15-year-old African-American girl, stood up for her rights. Claudette could sit only in the "colored" section of the bus. When the colored section was full and the "white-only" section was empty, Claudette had to stand. No African American was allowed to sit in front of or next to a white person. One day when all seats in the colored section were full, Claudette sat in the white-only section. When the bus driver told her to move, Claudette said, "It's my constitutional right to sit here." Claudette was arrested and taken to jail. This incident took place just a few months before Rosa Parks refused to move to the back of the bus. Perhaps Claudette's courage helped Rosa Parks in her act of courage.

   Key Word: _____   Number of Times It Appears: _____

LESSON 2

Taking Notes in Outline Form

Purpose

The purpose of this lesson is to introduce students to the skills of note-taking and developing outlines.

Materials Needed

⊛ set of three-hole-punched copies of Lesson 2 Student Pages (pages 14–19) for each student

⊛ four copies of the Paragraph Outline reproducible on page 14 for each student

⊛ overhead transparency of box on page 15, About Outline Form

Concepts to Be Taught

⊙ main topic

⊙ supporting details

⊙ outline form

Skills to Be Learned

Students will be able to read a paragraph, identify the main topic and supporting details, and write the topic and details in correct outline form.

Suggested Procedure

Distribute a set of Lesson 2 Student Pages to each student and the copies of the Paragraph Outline reproducible. Discuss Example 1 with students. Then, using the transparency, explain outline form to students. Explain that they will use this form when they're taking notes. Go over Examples 2 and 3. Then have students complete the Practice Paragraphs. You may wish to stop after the first paragraph and review students' completed outlines to make sure they understand how to reduce their notes to the fewest possible words. Be sure to tell students that they may not need to fill in a detail for every letter on the outline form, and that they may need to add letters for some paragraphs.

Follow-Up

Students may benefit from additional practice in reducing notes to the fewest words possible. Remind them to add Lesson 2 Student Pages to their binders.

Name _____ Date _____

Paragraph Outline

Use this page to take notes on paragraphs. You can also use this page to create an outline for paragraphs you plan to write. For some paragraphs you may not need to fill in all the detail lines. For others, you may need to add more lines.

   I. _____
       (Main topic)

     A. _____
        (Supporting detail)

     B. _____
        (Supporting detail)

     C. _____
        (Supporting detail)

     D. _____
        (Supporting detail)

Paragraph Writing Made Easy! Scholastic Professional Books

Name _____ Date _____

Taking Notes in Outline Form

Now that you can find the topic sentence in a paragraph, you're ready to organize the entire paragraph into the essential points of the main topic and supporting details using a process called note-taking.

Example 1: **Read the paragraph below.**

> Worker bees are tremendously busy. They gather nectar from the flower. They build the honeycombs. They feed and clean the queen bee. They also protect the hive.

The first sentence is the topic sentence. [**Hint:** When taking notes, you don't write the whole topic sentence. You reduce it to as few words as possible. For example, the sentence *Worker bees are tremendously busy* could be written as *Busy worker bees*.] So you might write:

Main topic: Busy worker bees

Next, find the sentences in the paragraph that give details or support the main topic. Ask yourself a question, such as "What do the worker bees do?" Then record your answer in the fewest possible words:

Main topic: Busy worker bees

Supporting details: Gather nectar
Build honeycombs
Feed and clean queen
Protect hive

About Outline Form

When information is put in outline form, it is organized in a certain way. Main topics are identified by using Roman numerals, and supporting information is identified with capital letters. When the "worker bees" paragraph is shown in outline form, it looks like this:

I. Busy worker bees
    A. Gather nectar
    B. Build honeycombs
    C. Feed and clean queen
    D. Protect hive

Name _____ Date _____

Example 2: **Let's look again at the birds paragraph (page 7) and use it as another note-taking example:**

Birds are animals with distinctive characteristics. For example, all birds have feathers. Birds also have beaks rather than teeth and wings instead of arms. In addition, birds lay eggs.

The first sentence is the topic sentence, and since it is the main topic, you reduce it to as few words as possible. So your notes might read, *Birds have distinctive characteristics.* The other sentences give supporting information about birds. When you take notes, you might write, *feathers, beaks, wings,* and *lay eggs.*

When you organize your notes into outline form, they will look like this:

**Main topic shown
with Roman numerals**

    I. Birds have distinctive characteristics

**Supporting details
shown with
capital letters**

    A. Feathers
    B. Beaks
    C. Wings
    D. Lay eggs

Paragraph Writing Made Easy! Scholastic Professional Books

Name _____ Date _____

Example 3: Read the following paragraph. Underline the topic sentence and reduce it to the fewest words possible.

Even though the tugboat is a small vessel, it has big jobs to perform. It helps to push and pull huge freighters and ocean liners in and out of city harbors. It helps maneuver large ships into their docks. It pulls barges in and out of the harbor and along the coast. It helps to lay telephone and television cables.

The topic sentence is the first sentence. When you take notes, reduce the topic to the fewest words possible:

Main topic: Small tugboats perform big jobs.

Next, you find the information in the paragraph that supports the main topic and reduce it to the fewest possible words. What jobs do small tugboats perform? List examples by taking information from each supporting sentence.

Write the main topic and the supporting details in outline form. Example:

    I. Small tugboats perform big jobs

        A. Push and pull huge ships

        B. Maneuver ships into docks

        C. Pull barges

        D. Lay communication cables

Name _____ Date _____

Practice Paragraphs

Read the following paragraphs and take your own notes. First, find and circle the key word or words. Underline the topic sentence. Using the topic sentence, ask yourself a question about the topic. Then take notes using copies of page 14.

1. Humpback whales are among the magnificent giants of the sea. These mammals average 45 feet in length. Their tail flukes are 12 feet wide. The humpback has about 30 throat grooves that allow its throat to expand. The humpback breathes through twin blowholes on top of its head. It seems playful as it leaps high into the air.

2. Walls and fences are often built to keep people out or to keep people in. The East German government built the Berlin Wall to prevent East German people from leaving their country. Prison walls are built to confine inmates to an enclosed, fortified space. The Great Wall of China, built to keep invaders out, has stood for 2,000 years and extends more than 1,500 miles.

Paragraph Writing Made Easy! Scholastic Professional Books

Name _____ Date _____

3. The behavior of chickadees at a feeding station is always interesting to watch. Although chickadees live in flocks, they come to the feeder one at a time. The dominant bird of the flock feeds first, while the other birds wait patiently, understanding their turns will come. The chickadee takes one seed at a time. This bird has great acrobatic abilities and can easily feed hanging upside down.

4. Heracles, a very popular Greek hero, accomplished incredible deeds of strength and bravery. He destroyed the ferocious Nemean lion with his bare hands. He killed the vicious, flesh-eating cranes with his bow and arrows. He was even able to descend into the land of the dead and capture Cerberus, the three-headed monster dog.

Supporting Sentence Review

Supporting sentences clarify the topic sentence of a paragraph by…

…giving additional information:	…giving examples:
Several things happened on the first day of school. Jane missed the bus, Joey forgot his notebook, and Alex went to the wrong homeroom.	Over time, birds' beaks have adapted to the way they find food. For example, the eagle has a hooked beak to catch…
…telling a story or incident:	**…showing events in chronological order:**
Rosa Parks's brave action helped to end bus segregation laws in the United States. One day in 1955 Rosa Parks refused to go to the back of the bus…	The lobster industry in Maine has changed dramatically over the past hundred years. In the old days lobstering was done by hand from a small rowboat. Later on, the lobstermen used sloops with big sails. Now, with gasoline engines, lobstermen can cover a much larger area in a short time.

Look back at Practice Paragraph 4 on page 5. In your own words, tell how the supporting sentences clarify or give further meaning to the topic sentence

LESSON 3

Outlines and Parallel Construction

Purpose

The purpose of this lesson is to introduce students to the concept of using parallel construction when developing outlines. Parallel construction means that subtopics begin with similar parts of speech—nouns, verbs, and so on. Parallel construction makes text more easily understood and assists students in converting notes to writing.

Concept to Be Taught

- parallel construction

Skills to Be Learned

Students will be able to read a paragraph and develop an outline that uses parallel construction, when appropriate.

Materials Needed

- set of three-hole-punched copies of Lesson 3 Student Pages (pages 21–22) for each student
- two copies of the Paragraph Outline reproducible on page 14

Suggested Procedure

Distribute a set of Lesson 3 Student Pages to each student. Use Examples 1 and 2 to explain parallel construction to students. Have students complete Practice Paragraphs 1 and 2. You may want to work with students to complete Practice Paragraph 1.

Follow-Up

You and your students can return to Lesson 2, Practice Paragraphs 1 through 4, for additional practice and reinforcement of the concept of parallel construction. Remind students to add the Lesson 3 Student Pages to their binders.

Name _____ Date _____

Outlines and Parallel Construction

When you write an outline, the first word of each supporting topic should be the same part of speech or grammatical construction. This pattern is called parallel construction. When using notes in outline form to construct a paragraph, putting the outline in parallel construction form makes the writing easier.

Example 1: **In the following outline of the topic, Heracles, each supporting topic or detail begins with a verb.**

> **I.** Heracles accomplished strong and brave deeds
> > **A.** *Destroyed* Nemean lion
> > **B.** *Killed* flesh-eating cranes
> > **C.** *Captured* three-headed dog, Cerberus

Whether you use verbs, nouns, adjectives, and so on to list subtopics, making the order consistent will simplify your organizational pattern and make writing easier. (Sometimes using parallel construction isn't possible. Then you'll have to find another way to organize the information. You'll find an example when you get to Student Page 18 in the paragraph about Maya Lin.)

Example 2: **Parallel construction can be used in different ways to create an outline. The following example uses adjectives and nouns instead of verbs at the start of each subtopic.**

> **I.** Heracles accomplished strong and brave deeds
> > **A.** *Nemean lions* destroyed
> > **B.** *Flesh-eating cranes* killed
> > **C.** *Three-headed dog*, Cerberus, captured

Name _____   Date _____

Practice Paragraphs

Read the following paragraphs. Underline the topic sentence and then take notes in outline form using copies of page 14. Use parallel construction.

1.   The great left-handed pitcher Steve Carlton felt that in order to pitch well he needed to eliminate all distractions. In his second year with the Philadelphia Phillies, he stopped talking to reporters. He also stopped reading newspapers. In addition, he stopped watching television. In order to focus only on his pitching, Mr. Carlton wanted no distractions from sportswriters.

2.   On a small island in New York Harbor stands the Statue of Liberty. The statue was a gift from the French government. She stands 305 feet tall. The statue holds the torch of freedom in her right hand. She holds a tablet dated July 4, 1776, in her left hand. She wears a crown with seven spikes that stand for the seven continents of the world.

LESSON 4

Signal Words

Purpose

Signal words are used by writers to make a transition from one idea to another. The purpose of this lesson is to show students how writers use signal words, how signal words can assist in comprehending text, and how signal words are useful in taking notes and developing outlines.

Materials Needed

⊛ set of three-hole-punched copies of Lesson 4 Student Pages (pages 24–29) for each student

⊛ overhead transparency of About Signal Words chart (page 24)

Suggested Procedure

Using an overhead projector and the transparency, work with your students to discuss the information on the chart, giving examples of the ways in which signal words signify certain kinds of information. Go over Examples 1 and 2. You may want to complete Practice Paragraph 1 with your students.

Follow-Up

Reinforce the concept of signal words by having students look for them as they read other material. Remind students to add the Lesson 4 materials to their binders.

Concepts to Be Taught

◉ signal words

◉ enumerative

◉ emphasizing

◉ sequence

◉ cause-effect

◉ comparison/contrast

◉ concluding/summarizing

Skill to Be Learned

Students will be able to identify signal words in a paragraph and describe how they are used.

Name _____ Date _____

About Signal Words

Signal words help the reader understand how the writer moves from one idea to another. Depending on how the ideas are arranged, the writer will use different words. Some frequently used signal words and the relationships they show are listed below.

enumerative	sequence	cause-effect
also	before	because
another	during	therefore
second	finally	thus
for example	at the start	consequently
furthermore	first	as a result of
in addition	last	
some	soon	**comparison/ contrast**
others	formerly	on the other hand
too	next	instead
likewise	then	however
a few	someday	different from
as well as	now	same as, similar to
	eventually	by contrast
emphasizing	when	unlike
mainly	whenever	although
most important	later	
chief	after	**concluding/ summarizing**
primarily	immediately	as a result
especially	long ago	in conclusion
	since	in summary
	today	

Name _____ Date _____

Signal Words

By pointing out a sequence or a change, signal words help organize a paragraph. Subtopic (supporting) details are emphasized by signal words such as *for example*, *therefore*, *as a result*, **and** *also*. **Watching for signal words will help you notice how the writer moves from point to point.**

Example 1: **Let's look again at the spiders paragraph (Example 5, page 9).**

> Spiders trap food in various ways. Some spiders make webs. Other spiders use a thread of silk like a lasso. Still other spiders live in the ground and come out to hunt. A few spiders live in flowers and camouflage themselves. Others live underwater and hunt at night.

The signal words are *some*, *other*, *still other*, *a few*, and *others*. These signal words introduce the five details. Circle the signal words. The following example shows how the signal words help you write the outline.

    I. Spiders trap food in various ways
        A. Make webs
        B. Make lasso
        C. Live in ground
        D. Live in flowers
        E. Live underwater

Name _____ Date _____

Example 2: Read the following paragraph about the discovery of ancient art. Signal words identify each work unearthed. Circle the signal words.

In the 1990s, near the village of Ufa on the steppes of southern Russia, Russian archeologists came upon a nomadic people's burial site. Digging into a large ancient earthen mound north of the Caspian Sea, the archeologists first discovered several wooden stags covered with layers of gold. These stags, with enlarged antlers, nose, and ears, are characteristic of the nomadic people's art and have been dated as early as the fourth century B.C. Second, the archeologists discovered solid gold images of wild sheep, perhaps used as weights for hanging textiles. The archeologists also unearthed silver and gold drinking vessels with enlarged ram-horn handles. In addition, the site revealed amphora, large earthenware vases with golden handles in the shape of rams, as well as spiral gold bracelets and necklaces. This discovery of the work of an ancient civilization has startled and thrilled the art world.

The main topic in this paragraph is at the beginning. The signal words *first, second, also, in addition*, and *as well as* help you identify the supporting details.

Example Outline:

    I. Discovery of nomadic burial site, near Ufa, fourth century B.C.

        A. Gold-covered stags

        B. Gold images of wild sheep

        C. Silver and gold drinking vessels

        D. Earthenware amphora with golden handles

        E. Gold bracelets and necklaces

Name _____ Date _____

Practice Paragraphs

Read the following paragraphs. Underline the topic sentence and circle the signal words. Then take notes in outline form on the lines provided. Try to use parallel construction. You may find that using parallel construction doesn't work easily. In such cases, be flexible and use your skills to organize the details as clearly and concisely as possible.

1. A good baseball catcher must develop particular skills. For example, she must be able to catch difficult pitches thrown through the batter's strike zone. Furthermore, she must be able to throw with accuracy and speed to catch a runner stealing. In addition, she must be able to tag out a runner charging into home while she is blocking the plate and holding on to the ball. Also, she must know each batter's weaknesses and tell the pitcher where to throw each pitch.

I. _____

   A. _____

   B. _____

   C. _____

   D. _____

Name _____ Date _____

2. Who would dream of winning a national architectural competition at the age of twenty-one? In 1980 Maya Ying Lin, a Chinese American, was chosen from among 1,400 artists to design the Vietnam Veterans Memorial in Washington, D.C. When she entered the competition, she was an architecture student at Yale University. She designed a 500-foot black granite V-shaped wall on which are carved the names of the 58,000 soldiers killed in the Vietnam War. At first, some people attacked the design because it was so different from traditional memorials. However, the memorial soon became deeply respected. Visitors touch, trace, and kiss the names on "The Wall." Over one million people visit the monument each year. As a result, Maya Lin has become a respected architect, chosen to design many other important memorials.

I. _____

  A. _____

  B. _____

  C. _____

  D. _____

  E. _____

  F. _____

Paragraph Writing Made Easy!   Scholastic Professional Books

Name _____ Date _____

3.   In 1969 a professional baseball player challenged a rule called the reserve clause, which allowed baseball owners to buy or sell players without their consent. That baseball player was Curtis Charles Flood. On October 7, 1969, the St. Louis Cardinals told Flood that he had been sold to the Philadelphia Phillies. Flood was shocked. He was in the prime of his career and had played for the Cardinals for 12 years. During the 1967 season, Flood broke records as a center fielder. Now he was to be sold. However, he refused; he said that he wasn't a piece of property to be bought and sold. Flood believed the reserve clause was illegal and immoral. He took the case to court, and eventually it went to the United States Supreme Court. In 1972 the court voted in favor of the baseball club owners. Although Curt Flood lost his battle, he paved the way for the defeat of the reserve clause. By the late 1970s players had options to choose the team on which they played.

I. _____

    A. _____

    B. _____

    C. _____

    D. _____

    E. _____

    F. _____

LESSON 5
Types of Paragraphs

Purpose

This lesson introduces students to different types of paragraphs that provide different types of information.

Materials Needed

- set of three-hole-punched copies of the Lesson 5 Student Pages (pages 31–41) for each student
- ten copies of the Paragraph Outline reproducible on page 14

Suggested Procedure

This lesson consists of five parts—one for each type of paragraph. Each type is first presented with one or two Examples followed by two Practice Paragraphs. First, distribute the Student Pages on the enumerative paragraph, and go over the examples. Allow time for questions and discussion. Then have students work on the Practice Paragraphs independently. Proceed with the sequence paragraph, and so on. You will probably want to divide the material in Lesson 5 into five class periods—one for each type of paragraph.

Follow-Up

After presenting the material in this lesson, have students try writing one paragraph of each type. This practice will reinforce what students have learned and will begin to prepare them for the material in Section 2. Remind students to add the Lesson 5 Student Pages to their binders.

Concepts to Be Taught

Characteristics of the various kinds of paragraphs:

- ◉ enumerative
- ◉ sequence
- ◉ cause-effect
- ◉ comparison/contrast
- ◉ descriptive

Skills to Be Learned

Students will be able to identify the five types of paragraphs and the kind of information presented by each. They'll be able to develop outlines from each kind of paragraph.

Name_____ Date _____

Types of Paragraphs

This lesson introduces five types of paragraphs: *enumerative, sequence, cause-effect, comparison/contrast,* and *descriptive.* Identifying different types of paragraphs will help you to understand what you read and to organize what you write. Remember to watch for signal words. They can help you outline the paragraph.

The Enumerative Paragraph

In an enumerative paragraph, a writer develops the paragraph by using examples. The specific focus of the paragraph is stated in the topic sentence and is followed by several supporting examples. Signal words, such as *for example, first, furthermore,* and *also* tell the reader that another example is coming up in the paragraph. Refer back to page 24 for other signal words often used in enumerative paragraphs.

Example 1: Here is an example of an enumerative paragraph.

> Walls are built for different purposes. For example, Hadrian's Wall was built in 125 A.D. across the neck of Scotland to keep the northern Picts out of newly acquired Roman territory in England. Another example is a pasture wall, built to keep livestock safe and protected. A third kind of wall is a memorial wall. The Vietnam Veterans Memorial wall was completed in 1982 and displays the names of that war's dead and missing. Finally, the most common use of walls, of course, is in housing to separate rooms and to support roofs.

The topic is walls. The topic sentence is: *Walls are built for different purposes.* The writer mentions several examples of different types of walls and their uses. The types and their purposes are flagged by the signal words: *for example, another example, a third,* and *finally.* An outline of the paragraph might look like this:

I. Purposes of walls

    A. Defense—Hadrian's Wall

    B. Protection—pasture wall

    C. Memorial—Vietnam Veterans Memorial

    D. Support—house walls

Now go on to Practice Paragraphs 1 and 2 to reinforce what you've learned.

Name _____ Date _____

Practice Paragraphs—Enumerative

Read the following enumerative paragraphs. Underline the topic sentences. Circle the signal words. Then take notes in outline form using copies of page 14. Try to use parallel construction.

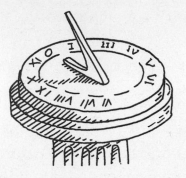

1. Over the centuries, many different kinds of timepieces have been developed. For example, one of the earliest clocks was the sundial, used in Egypt thousands of years ago. Another clock, used at a later time, was the English pendulum clock, which uses weights to move gears. It is still used today and is known as the grandfather clock. More modern examples of timepieces are the wristwatch, which uses springs, and the digital clock that uses batteries. Further examples may be developed in the future, using nuclear energy and other sources of energy. People everywhere have always created ways to measure time.

2. What qualities do you think make a great leader? For instance, a leader needs to know how to solve problems. A leader also needs to surround him or herself with competent people. Perhaps most important, a leader needs to have a vision of the future. Furthermore, a leader needs to persuade others to share that vision and to inspire others to follow. Who do you think is a great leader?

Paragraph Writing Made Easy! Scholastic Professional Books

Name _____ Date _____

The Sequence Paragraph

A sequence paragraph presents information in a certain order. The author may be telling you how to do or make something, or may be presenting information in a time sequence. The detail sentences in a sequence paragraph must be in a particular order. If the order is changed, the paragraph will be difficult to understand.

Example 1: **Here is an example of a sequence paragraph.**

> Before a batter comes to bat during a baseball game, he first selects his favorite bat from a rack in the dugout. He then moves into the batter's circle, which is located between the dugout and home plate. As he goes to the plate, he swings his bat with a weight on it or swings two bats. Next, he kneels in the batter's circle and watches the pitcher intently. When it is his turn, he strides forward to the plate and positions himself in the batter's box. Finally, he faces the pitcher, adjusts his cap, takes a final swing of the bat, and waits for the first pitch. As you can see, a batter goes through several steps in preparation for coming to bat.

The last sentence in the paragraph, *As you can see, a batter goes through several steps in preparation for coming to bat,* is the topic sentence. You may have noticed that the writer helped organize the detail sentences in the paragraph by using signal words that you learned about on page 24. In this case the signal words are *first, then, as, next, when,* and *finally.* Use the lines below to take notes in outline form.

I. _____

    A. _____

    B. _____

    C. _____

    D. _____

    E. _____

    F. _____

Now go on to the Practice Paragraphs to reinforce what you've learned about sequence paragraphs.

Practice Paragraphs—Sequence

Read the sequence paragraphs. Use copies of page 14 to take notes. Remember: the signal words will help you. Try to use parallel construction.

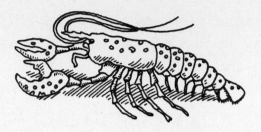

1.   The lobster industry in Maine has changed dramatically over the past hundred years. In the old days lobstering was done by hand from a small rowboat close to the shoreline. Later on, the lobstermen used Friendship sloops with big sails, enabling them to fish farther out. Now, with the introduction of the gasoline engine, a much larger area can be covered in a short time.

Sometimes when a story is told, dates are used to move from one event to another. In this case, dates behave like signal words.

2.   Justice Thurgood Marshall was an outstanding lawyer and a crusader for racial justice. He graduated from Howard University's all-black law school in 1933. He then began working for the admission of blacks to all-white law schools. After winning a case to end segregation at the University of Maryland's law school, Marshall soon went on to fight segregation policies in all-white public high schools and elementary schools. Eventually, in 1954, his greatest legal victory was the Supreme Court's decision *Brown vs. the Board of Education* to end segregation in all public schools throughout the country. Marshall was appointed to the Supreme Court in 1967 and was considered by many to be the moral and social conscience of the court. Justice Marshall died on January 24, 1993.

Name _____ Date _____

The Cause-Effect Paragraph

A third type of paragraph is the cause-effect paragraph. The supporting sentences in a cause-effect paragraph show the effects, or results, of something that happened.

The phrases *because of, therefore*, **and** *as a result of* **are examples of signal words found in cause-effect paragraphs. See page 24 for others.**

Example 1: **Here is an example of a cause-effect paragraph.**

> In 1988 a destructive earthquake hit San Francisco. Buildings rocked on their foundations, and some collapsed. Gas mains ruptured causing fires to break out in several parts of the city. Telephone and electric service was cut off. Worst of all, roads and highways buckled, killing a large number of people in automobiles and trucks.

The topic sentence is: *In 1988 a destructive earthquake hit San Francisco.* The supporting sentences show the effects of the destructive earthquake. Use the lines below to take notes in outline form.

I. _____

    A. _____

    B. _____

    C. _____

    D. _____

Go on to the Practice Paragraphs to reinforce what you've learned about cause-effect paragraphs.

Name _____   Date _____

Practice Paragraphs—Cause-Effect

Read the following cause-effect paragraphs. Underline the topic sentence. Then take notes in outline form using copies of page 14. Try to use parallel construction.

1. Many kinds of birds are endangered today because of irresponsible human behavior. The conversion of short-grass prairie wetlands to agricultural lands has destroyed the habitats of many waterfowl. Oil and chemical spills in seacoast areas kill thousands of seabirds and destroy nesting sites. Cutting trees to make housing developments and commercial areas often disturbs the breeding grounds of songbirds. The effect of changes by human beings to what was once wild habitat has resulted in a decrease in bird population.

2. The sinking of the "unsinkable" *Titanic* was one of the great sea disasters. The ocean liner *Titanic* left Southampton, England, for New York on her maiden voyage in April 1912. On April 14 icebergs were sighted. Later that night, at 11:40 P.M., while grown-ups danced and children slept, the *Titanic* collided with an iceberg. It ripped a 300-foot gash in the bow. Lifeboats saved only one-half of the ship's passengers and crew. As a result of extreme negligence at sea, the *Titanic* sank and 1,500 people drowned. The unnecessary loss of life was an international calamity.

Paragraph Writing Made Easy! Scholastic Professional Books

Name _____ Date _____

The Comparison/Contrast Paragraph

The fourth type of paragraph is the comparison/contrast paragraph. Signal words such as *different from*, *same as*, *unlike*, and *similar* give you clues to a comparison/contrast paragraph. The topic sentence names the subjects that are to be compared or contrasted, and the supporting sentences tell how the subjects are alike (comparison) or different (contrast).

Example 1: **Here is an example of a *comparison* paragraph. The supporting sentences tell how the subjects are alike.**

Bicycle and ski racers need physical and mental strength and extraordinary endurance. The racers must be physically fit. They also both need total control of their bike or skis. In addition, they must think ahead and be prepared for a possible spur-of-the-moment tactic. They are further alike in that they need perseverance to continue a race when feeling stress or suffering from an injury. Finally, they need the determination to succeed. Bicycle and ski racers have similar needs.

The topic sentence is: *Bicycle and ski racers need physical and mental strength and extraordinary endurance.* The signal words *also, in addition, further,* and *finally* point to the supporting sentences that explain the similarities. An outline might look like this:

I. Bicycle racers and ski racers—primary needs

    A. Physical fitness

    B. Total control of bike or skis

    C. Planned tactics

    D. Perseverance under stress and injury

    E. Determination to succeed

Name _____ Date _____

Example 2: **Following is an example of a *contrast* paragraph. The supporting sentences tell how the subjects, in this case birds, are different.**

Birds have different kinds of feet in order to fulfill certain needs. For example, ducks have webbed feet in order to swim easily. By contrast, eagles have feet with curved claws in order to grasp their prey. Chickadees have feet with three toes pointing forward and one toe pointing backward, to enable them to hold on to branches. On the other hand, wading birds such as herons have long pointed feet, to stir up the muddy bottom of rivers and streams.

The topic sentence is: *Birds have different kinds of feet in order to fulfill certain needs.* The signal words *for example, by contrast,* and *on the other hand* provide clues to those differences. An outline of the paragraph might look like this:

I. Examples of birds' feet

A. Ducks, webbed for swimming

B. Eagles, curved for grasping

C. Chickadees, toes forward and backward for holding

D. Herons, pointed and long for digging

Now go on to the Practice Paragraphs to reinforce what you've learned about compare/contrast paragraphs.

Name _____ Date _____

Practice Paragraphs– Compare/Contrast

Read the following paragraphs. Underline the topic sentence. Circle the signal words. Then take notes in outline form using copies of page 14. Try to use parallel construction.

1.   People everywhere—regardless of culture, religion, race, sex, or age—possess many of the same needs. First, we all need music—music to hear, compose, play, or sing. We need music to survive and flourish. In addition, we all need to learn to be good neighbors, to help each other in times of trouble or grief. Furthermore, we all need the freedom to define ourselves, to say who we are and speak up for ourselves. These three needs are important to all people of the world.

2.   The most difficult position on a baseball team is that of catcher, and most of us loyal fans assume that the position requires a strong if not burly male. For example, Yogi Berra, Carlton Fisk, Roy Campanella, and Johnny Bench are names that come to mind. However, how many fans know about our professional women baseball catchers? During World War II, professional women catchers, such as Dorothy "Dottie" Green and Mary Rountree, played behind home plate with vigor and skill. When talking about baseball, we must not forget the women who played in the 1940s.

Name _____ Date _____

The Descriptive Paragraph

Authors write a descriptive paragraph when they want to tell the reader what something is, or how something looks, tastes, smells, or feels. The topic sentence in a descriptive paragraph presents the subject that is being described. The supporting sentences actually describe the subject in detail.

Example 1: **This paragraph about the Statue of Liberty is a descriptive paragraph.**

On a small island in New York Harbor stands the Statue of Liberty. The statue was a gift from the French government. She stands 305 feet tall. The statue holds the torch of freedom in her right hand. She holds a tablet dated July 4, 1776, in her left hand. She wears a crown with seven spikes that stand for the seven continents of the world.

You can see that the topic sentence *On a small island in New York Harbor stands the Statue of Liberty* presents what is going to be described. The other sentences, the detail sentences, describe, or tell you about, the Statue of Liberty. Now take notes in outline form.

   I. _____

     A. _____

     B. _____

     C. _____

     D. _____

     E. _____

Now go on to the Practice Paragraphs to reinforce what you've learned about descriptive paragraphs.

Name _____ Date _____

Practice Paragraphs–Descriptive

Read the following paragraphs. They are descriptive paragraphs. Underline the topic sentence, then take notes in outline form using the copies of page 14. Try to use parallel construction.

1.   Scientists found a baby dinosaur nest in Montana in the 1980s. The nest was three feet deep and six feet wide, and it contained several baby dinosaur skeletons. The babies were three feet long and thought to be two months old. Scientists believed that the babies were related to the duck-billed dinosaurs, which lived more than 60 million years ago.

2.   The dolphin belongs to a group of mammals called cetaceans. They breathe air, have warm blood, and give birth to live baby dolphins. Dolphins grow to 12 feet in length and can weigh over 400 pounds. They have no fur and no hind legs. Dolphins are very agile. They dive as deep as 70 feet and leap as high as 30 feet. They can stay underwater for 15 minutes. The dolphin cannot smell but has excellent hearing. Because most species of dolphin possess a high level of animal intelligence, they can be trained to perform many complicated maneuvers on command.

LESSON 6

More Detailed Outline Form

Purpose

The purpose of this lesson is to encourage students to include more details in their notes and to enable them to incorporate those details into their outlines.

Materials Needed

⊛ set of three-hole-punched copies of Lesson 6 Student Pages (pages 43–50) for each student

⊛ overhead transparency of About the More Detailed Outline Form on page 43

⊛ five copies of the Detailed Outline for Paragraphs reproducible on page 43

Concepts to Be Taught

◉ supporting details

◉ additional details

◉ outline form

Skills to Be Learned

Students will be able to identify details that support and give additional information about a topic. They will learn to develop outlines that include both supporting and additional details.

Suggested Procedure

Using an overhead projector and the transparency discuss the detailed outline form with students and explain how it differs from the outline form used up to this point. Work with students to complete the example Paragraphs on page 45 and 46. It is also important to work closely with your students on the first few Practice Paragraphs in this lesson.

Follow-Up

Remind students to place the Lesson 6 Student Pages in their binders.

Name _____ Date _____

Detailed Outline for Paragraphs

Use this page to take more detailed notes on paragraphs. You can also use this page to create a more detailed outline for paragraphs you plan to write. Using the More Detailed Outline Form on pages 44 and 45 as your guide, create an outline form that fits the paragraph you are reading.

I. _____

_____

_____

_____

_____

_____

_____

_____

_____

_____

_____

_____

_____

_____

_____

_____

_____

Name _____ Date _____

More Detailed Outline Form

Making an outline of a topic puts the ideas in their correct order and shows which ideas are the most important. Up to this point, you've made outlines that show the main topic and the most important supporting information. However, some paragraphs contain more detailed information that you'll want to include in your outline. After you select the main topic, you may find you need more than one subtopic. You also may want to add specific examples or more details about the subtopic. In these cases you need to learn to use a more detailed outline form.

About the More Detailed Outline Form

When information is put in a more detailed outline form, it is organized in a certain way. As you've already learned, main topics are identified with Roman numerals and subtopics are identified with capital letters. The supporting details to the subtopics are identified by regular numerals (1, 2, 3, and so on). Then additional details for the supporting details are identified by lowercase letters (a, b, c, and so on).

    I. Main topic

      A. Subtopic

        1. Supporting detail

        2. Supporting detail

          a. Additional detail

          b. Additional detail

          c. Additional detail

      B. Subtopic

        1. Supporting detail

        2. Supporting detail

          a. Additional detail

        3. Supporting detail

Paragraph Writing Made Easy! Scholastic Professional Books

Example 1: Read the following paragraph.

Long ago, Persia, now called Iran, supplied the world with many useful and beautiful products. Some of the products were foods. For example, pistachio nuts were used to flavor tea and desserts. Fruits such as the peach, apricot, and fig all came from Persia. Other products were textiles. Persia's delicate silk, rich brocades, and magnificent oriental rugs, were prized possessions throughout the world.

The first sentence is the topic sentence. As you read about the products from Persia, you will see that they can be divided into categories. The first four products are food and the last three are textiles. Two signal words—*some* and *other*—help you understand that there are two categories of products. See below for a more detailed outline form for the paragraph.

Main topic	**I.** Persia gave many products to the world
Subtopic	**A.** Foods
Supporting detail	**1.** Pistachio nuts
Supporting detail	**2.** Fruits
Additional detail	**a.** Peaches
Additional detail	**b.** Apricots
Additional detail	**c.** Figs
Subtopic	**B.** Textiles
Supporting detail	**1.** Silk
Supporting detail	**2.** Brocades
Supporting detail	**3.** Oriental rugs

The more detailed outline makes a picture in diagram form of the main topic and supporting topics and uses numbers and letters to clarify the picture.

Name _____ Date _____

Example 2: **Read the following paragraph. Find the topic sentence. Circle the signal words.**

One of our nation's most active first ladies, Eleanor Roosevelt, not only learned of the social problems that existed during her day, but she also publicized them. First, she found the nation's youth unable to get jobs. She discovered that African Americans were the last to be hired. She found women unable to apply for many jobs because they were reserved for men only. She learned that tenant farmers, the homeless, and minorities were without a spokesperson. Second, Mrs. Roosevelt was determined to speak out against social injustices. She held regularly scheduled press conferences and wrote a daily syndicated newspaper column called "My Day." By telling the true story of the forgotten, she brought relief to millions of people.

In this paragraph the main topic is in the first sentence. Two signal words, *first* and *second*, introduce two supporting subtopics and thus help you organize the paragraph in outline form. In this more detailed outline, each subtopic is supported by details.

I. First Lady Eleanor Roosevelt learned of and publicized social problems

    A. Learned of social problems

        1. Youth unemployment

        2. African Americans last hired

        3. Women overlooked for many jobs—men only

        4. Tenant farmers, homeless, minorities—no spokesperson

    B. Publicized social problems

        1. Held press conferences

        2. Wrote daily newspaper column, "My Day"

Name _____ Date _____

Practice Paragraphs

Read the following paragraphs. Underline the topic sentence. Circle the signal words. Then take notes using copies of page 43. Try to use parallel construction.

1. When our founding fathers wrote the Bill of Rights, they wrote about rights and responsibilities. First of all, this bill stated that every person has certain rights. The Bill of Rights includes such rights as freedom of speech, freedom to practice religion, freedom to buy property, freedom to have trial by jury, and freedom to vote. Second, we citizens have responsibilities. Citizens have responsibilities to vote, to serve on juries, and to write letters to the president and representatives in Congress. Citizens have responsibilities to protest injustices and to improve life in their communities.

2. The Wabanakis (Wah/buh/nah/keys), the native people who lived in the area now called New England, suffered greatly from diseases brought by European settlers. For example, they had no immunity to diseases, such as measles, scarlet fever, and smallpox. Furthermore, they could no longer rely on traditional methods to cure themselves. Herbal medicines, such as teas made from goldenrod or powders made from roots, often did not work. In addition, the medicine man's treatments were now ineffective against these unknown contagious diseases. The community of Wabanakis, formerly self-sufficient, found it difficult to care for itself. Although the Wabanaki tribe as a nation was destroyed by disease and wars, its people have survived to this day.

Name _____ Date _____

3.   Since dams built across large rivers prevent fish from returning to spawning grounds upstream, two kinds of apparatus have been developed to help the fish. The first of these is a fish ladder. This ladder consists of a series of platforms from the base of the dam to the top. These platforms are four to five feet high. Water flowing down them creates small waterfalls. Fish such as salmon and trout are capable of jumping these distances against the falling water and are thus able to jump and swim from the bottom of the dam to the top and to the lake beyond. The second device is the fish lift. This lift is a bargelike container in the water at the foot of the dam. Thousands of fish, such as shad and herring, swim into the container. Unable to jump the way other fish can, they rely on these fish lifts, which are hydraulically raised. The fish are then transferred into trucks and taken upstream to spawning grounds.

Paragraph Writing Made Easy! Scholastic Professional Books

Name _____ Date _____

4.   Biologist Rachel Carson was a woman of great vision and courage. From the time she was a young child, she loved the fish in the sea and the animals on land. With her teachers she examined the barnacle and periwinkle, the earthworm and honeybee. Later, as a graduate student, she studied biology at the Marine Biological Laboratory in Woods Hole, Massachusetts, and genetics at Johns Hopkins University. Then, as a biologist, Carson worked for the United States Bureau of Fisheries and the Fish and Wildlife Service. However, in 1952 she left her job because she was distressed by the many chemicals being used as pesticides. She devoted all of her time to the study of synthetic insecticides and their effect on land, rivers, and the sea. She discovered that these deadly chemicals poisoned all plant and wildlife as well as humans. As a result of her research, she wrote the book *Silent Spring* in 1962. The book sent shock waves through the health and environmental communities. It led to the establishment of the federal Environmental Protection Agency and the banning of the most dangerous insecticides. Rachel Carson, through her courageous dedication, helped save the world from a global environmental disaster.

Name _____ Date _____

5.   The experience of two different cultures in earlier periods
might offer helpful models for alleviating some of the problems of
families today. First, in the seventeenth century the Iroquois
Indians lived in large extended family units. The mother, father,
children, grandparents, aunts, uncles, and cousins all lived
together in a single space. This family group ate, worked, and
played together. Everyone shared responsibilities. The whole
family learned to contribute to the good of the community.
Second, in the mid-nineteenth century Jewish families living in
Palestine began to build communities in the desert. The adults
worked in the fields and also cared for and taught the children.
The children had daily school classes and daily jobs. From a young
age, the children, like the Native American children, shared
responsibilities and learned to work for the good of the
community. These two cultures used all family members to work
in unified ways for the well-being of the community.

LESSON 7

Using Notes to Write Paragraphs

Purpose

The purpose of this lesson is to teach students how to use their own words to convert notes they've taken into well-constructed paragraphs. This is the most important lesson in this section. Students must not only construct complete sentences from their notes, but also learn to expand and embellish these sentences so that the result is interesting and conveys complete information. Students also must learn how to write a concluding sentence.

Concepts to Be Taught

- ◉ expanding notes
- ◉ embellishing basic information
- ◉ clincher (concluding sentence)

Skills to Be Learned

Students will be able to write complete and expanded sentences from notes. They will be able to write a clincher (a concluding sentence).

Materials Needed

❀ set of three-hole-punched copies of the Lesson 7 Student Pages (pages 53–56) for each student

Suggested Procedure

Distribute a set of Student Pages to each student. With your students study the introductory information provided. For example, point out that the outline about tugboats uses as few words as possible. Explain that students will convert these few words into expanded sentences that give details and are interesting to read. Thus, the notes in Subtopic A, *Push and pull huge ships,* may become, *The tugboat helps to push and pull huge freighters and ocean liners in and out of city harbors.*

Because writing notes will help students to comprehend and remember text they read earlier, many will recall these details as they use their note-taking skills to write reports and other assignments. Some students may not remember. When students are writing reports, they will be able to add to their original notes by referring back to the source of their notes. Students can also add to their original notes through class discussions, individual conversations with classmates or a teacher, or using reference books to embellish their writing.

In addition each paragraph needs a concluding sentence. The Clincher box on page 54 presents students with the concept of writing a concluding sentence for the paragraph.

Since the skill of using notes to write paragraphs is so important, you'll want to give students extra practice before they continue with the Practice Outlines that follow.

Follow-Up

With your students, return to the Practice Paragraphs in previous lessons to reinforce the concept of the clincher. Remind students to put the Lesson 7 Student Pages in their binders. Students can self-correct, which will help them gain confidence.

Name _____ Date _____

Using Notes to Write Paragraphs

Do you remember the notes on tugboats in Section 1 (page 17)?

   I. Small tugboats perform big jobs
      A. Push and pull huge ships
      B. Maneuver ships into docks
      C. Pull barges
      D. Lay communication cables

Using these notes, you can now begin to construct a paragraph. The first step is to write a topic sentence—the one sentence that presents the topic to be discussed in the paragraph.

Example 1: **Read the notes and extract the most important words and ideas that describe the tugboat. Then form the topic sentence.**

   Even though the tugboat is a small boat, it has many big jobs to perform.

Next, since there are four details given in the outline—A, B, C, and D—you can write four detail sentences to support the topic sentence.

   The tugboat helps to push and pull huge freighters and ocean liners in and out of city harbors.

   The tugboat helps maneuver large ships into their docks.

   The tugboat pulls barges in and out of the harbor and along the coast.

   The tugboat helps to lay telephone and television cables.

Now combine the topic sentence and the detail sentences, and add some signal words and a concluding sentence at the end. You will then have a well-constructed paragraph about the tugboat's jobs.

_____

_____

_____

_____

_____

Name _____ Date _____

Even though the tugboat is a small boat, it has big jobs to perform. For example, the tugboat helps to push and pull huge freighters and ocean liners in and out of city harbors. It helps maneuver large ships into their docks. Also, it pulls barges in and out of the harbor and along the coast. In addition, tugboats help to lay telephone and television cables. The tugboat, though small, is very powerful.

The Clincher

You have learned that the purpose of a well-constructed paragraph is to help the reader understand the subject under discussion. You have also learned that good paragraphs have a topic sentence and supporting details. In addition, many paragraphs also have another kind of sentence called the clincher. The clincher is usually, but not always, the last sentence in the paragraph. It is a concluding sentence and restates in different words the topic or the specific focus of the paragraph. A well-written paragraph usually has a clincher. The clincher sentence in the paragraph about tugboats is *The tugboat, though small, is very powerful.*

Paragraph Writing Made Easy! Scholastic Professional Books

Name _____ Date _____

Practice Outlines

1. **Imagine that you have taken notes and made an outline on the humpback whale.**

   I. Humpback whales are sea giants
   - **A.** Mammals
   - **B.** Length, 45 feet
   - **C.** Tail flukes, 12 feet wide, used for propelling
   - **D.** Throat, 30 expanding grooves used for feeding
   - **E.** Blowholes, used for breathing
   - **F.** Leap high in air

Take a few moments to study the outline. Notice the details.

What is the main topic?

_____

How many details support the main topic?

_____

If you don't know much about humpback whales, take some time now to increase your knowledge. Because you don't have the original text, you may wish to discuss humpbacks with your teacher or a classmate. Or you may want to use a reference book to find additional information about these whales.

Using the outline and the additional information you have learned, what would be a good topic sentence for a paragraph about humpback whales? Write the sentence here.

_____

_____

Then write six detail sentences telling about the six subtopics in the outline. Include a clincher sentence. Use a separate sheet of paper to write your paragraph.

After you've written your paragraph, turn to page 18. Does your paragraph look something like the one on that page? It is an example of a descriptive paragraph. The topic sentence is: *Humpback whales are among the magnificent giants of the sea.* The clincher is: *The humpback seems playful as it leaps high into the air.*

LESSON 7: Using Notes to Write Paragraphs

Name _____ Date _____

2. **Read and study the outline below.**

    I. Different kinds of timepieces

        A. Sundial—Egypt, uses sun

        B. Grandfather clock, uses weights

        C. Wristwatch, uses springs

        D. Digital clock, uses batteries

        E. Possible future clocks, using nuclear energy

The outline is organized with a main topic and five details. The details are examples selected to support the main topic.

    Now write a paragraph about this topic. First, write the topic sentence. Support your topic sentence with the five examples listed in the outline. Use one sentence for each example. As you write, think of a good clincher.

_____

_____

_____

_____

_____

_____

_____

_____

_____

_____

Now turn to page 32. Does your paragraph look something like the paragraph on that page? This is an example of an enumerative paragraph. It uses examples. It includes four signal words. Can you find them?

Paragraph Writing Made Easy! Scholastic Professional Books

LESSON 8
Using Signal Words

Purpose

This lesson reviews the concept of signal words, which was introduced in Section 1, Lesson 4. However, instead of using signal words to comprehend and take notes on text, students will use them to construct well-organized paragraphs with strong supporting sentences.

Materials Needed

◉ three-hole-punched copies of Lesson 8 Student Pages (pages 58–64) for each student

◉ overhead transparency of Signal Words, page 24

Concept to Be Taught

◉ signal words as writing devices

Skill to Be Learned

Students will be able to use signal words to show the relationship of supporting sentences to the topic of a paragraph.

Suggested Procedure

Distribute a set of Student Pages to each student. Use the Signal Words transparency to review the concept. Then review the types of paragraphs (Section 1, Lesson 5) and how signal words provide a transition to the supporting sentences, which give additional information about the topic. Using Examples 1 and 2 with your students, practice using signal words to write paragraphs. Depending on how your students are progressing, you'll have to decide how many paragraphs to complete in one class session and when to let students work independently. One paragraph may be enough to start. This will give you and your students time to discuss how best to write the assigned paragraph.

Follow-Up

You'll need to review and evaluate the Practice Paragraphs students wrote on their own. Use your findings to identify weaknesses and provide extra help. Remember: the answers provided on page 80 are only suggestions.

Name _____ Date _____

Using Signal Words

You learned that *signal words* help organize a paragraph by pointing out a sequence or a change (Section 1, Lesson 4). You also saw that signal words such as *for example*, *therefore*, *as a result*, and *also* introduce or emphasize supporting details (subtopics).

In studying Section 1, you noticed signal words used in paragraphs throughout the text. Take a moment to look again at Practice Paragraph 1 on page 39. In the paragraph about people all over the world who have many of the same needs, three signal words are used to introduce three important subtopics. The signal words *first*, *in addition*, and *furthermore* organize the paragraph to help the reader understand and remember it. The three signal words point out and emphasize three important needs that all people share. The signal word list will help you select and use the appropriate signals for your paragraphs.

Example 1: Read the following outline and study the information about migrating birds. Then write a topic sentence, the one sentence that tells what the paragraph is about. Next, add supporting sentences. Use signal words. Finally, add a clincher sentence at the end.

    I. Distances flown by migrating birds to nesting grounds

        A. Sanderling—8,000 miles from central Chile to northeast Greenland

        B. Whooping crane—4,000 miles, coastal Texas to northwest Canada

        C. Arctic tern—16,000 miles, circumpolar, from pole to pole

_____

_____

_____

_____

_____

Turn to the next page to see a sample topic sentence and paragraph.

LESSON 8: Using Signal Words

Name _____ Date _____

Topic Sentence:

Some migrating birds fly extraordinary distances to their nesting grounds.

Sample Paragraph:

Some migrating birds fly extraordinary distances to their nesting grounds. For example, the small sanderling flies 8,000 miles from central Chile to northeast Greenland. Another bird, the tall North American whooping crane, flies 4,000 miles from coastal Texas to northwest Canada. Even more amazing, the Arctic tern flies 16,000 miles from the Arctic Ocean to the Antarctic seas. These migrating birds seem unbelievable to us as they fly great distances to breed.

Were your topic sentence and paragraph something like these?

Name _____ Date _____

Example 2: Read the following outline and study the information about Native Americans. Then write a paragraph. First, write a topic sentence. Next, add supporting sentences. Use signal words. Finally, add a clincher.

I. Native Americans often misrepresented by glib stereotypes

    A. Mascots and symbols—not living people

    B. ABC picture books—"I is for Indian"

    C. Children's books—animals dressed in "Indian suits"

    D. Children's Halloween costumes—feathered headdresses, a sacred symbol

    E. Sports teams named Cleveland Indians, Atlanta Braves, Washington Redskins

_____

_____

_____

_____

_____

_____

_____

_____

_____

_____

_____

_____

Turn the page to see a sample topic sentence and paragraph.

Name _____ Date _____

Topic Sentence:

Native Americans often appear as mascots and symbols rather than as living people with rich and diverse cultures.

Sample Paragraph:

Native Americans often are misrepresented by glib stereotypes. They appear as mascots and symbols rather than as living people. For example, ABC books sometimes show "I is for Indian." In addition, many children's books show pictures of animals dressed in "Indian suits." Likewise, as a dress-up for Halloween, children wear feathered headdresses, a sacred symbol for some native peoples. Furthermore, sports teams are named the Cleveland Indians, Atlanta Braves, and Washington Redskins, without concern that the names might offend Native Americans. Today many people are distressed that mascots, symbols, and team names are used to represent Native Americans, which is not respectful of the rich and diverse cultures of these peoples.

Compare your paragraph with this one. Did you include all the important information?

Name _____ Date _____

Practice Outlines

1. Read the following outline and study the information describing how the Ojibway people lived. Then write a paragraph. Begin by writing a topic sentence. Next, add supporting sentences. Use signal words when appropriate. Finish your paragraph with a clincher.

    I. Ojibway people—respected land and all living things

        A. Lived on land now Minnesota

        B. Shared land with each other and with animals

        C. Considered trees a sacred gift

        D. Cut just enough wood, roots, and bark to build lodges

        E. Killed those animals needed for food and clothing

        F. Careful not to waste

_____

_____

_____

_____

_____

_____

_____

_____

_____

_____

_____

Paragraph Writing Made Easy! Scholastic Professional Books

Name _____ Date _____

2. **Here is another outline to change into a paragraph. Study the outline.**

    I. Young Anne Frank, a Jew, hid to escape persecution by Nazis, World War II

        A. Lived in secret attic apartment, father's Amsterdam business building, two years

        B. Helped by four of Mr. Frank's employees

        C. Made noise only when warehouse empty

        D. Given hope by news on radio

        E. Celebrated birthdays and Jewish holidays

        F. Continued to study and learn

        G. Betrayed by an unknown person, August 1944

        H. Taken to concentration camp

        I. Died of typhus, in camp, April 1945

Is the central idea of the outline expressed in the main topic? If so, the main topic can be changed into a topic sentence.

Now write your paragraph. Remember that when a story is told, dates are used to move from one event to the other. In this way, dates are like signal words.

_____

_____

_____

_____

_____

_____

_____

_____

_____

_____

Name _____ Date _____

3. Read the following outline and study the information about the marathon. Then write a paragraph. First, write a topic sentence. Next, add supporting sentences. Use the dates in sequence to help you organize the supporting sentences. Finally, write a clincher.

    I. Development of the marathon

        A. 490 B.C., a Greek soldier ran from the battlefield of Marathon to Athens, 22 miles, to tell of victory of Greeks over Persians

        B. 1896, first modern marathon, Greece, a race from Marathon to Athens

        C. 1897, first American marathon, Boston, 25 miles

        D. 1908, marathon distance increased to 26 miles for Olympic Games in England

        E. 1970, New York marathon, 127 runners

        F. Today, city marathons, many thousands of runners

_____

_____

_____

_____

_____

_____

_____

_____

_____

_____

_____

_____

_____

Paragraph Writing Made Easy! Scholastic Professional Books

LESSON 9

Using the More Detailed Outline Form for Writing

Purpose

This review teaches students to include more descriptive and detailed information in their writing.

Materials Needed

⊛ three-hole-punched copies of the Lesson 9 Student Pages (pages 66–73)

Suggested Procedure

Distribute a set of Student Pages to each student. Use an overhead projector to review the More Detailed Outline Form and explain to students how the additional detail makes topics more informative and interesting to the reader. Work together to complete Examples 1 and 2. Students will need extra sheets of paper to write their paragraphs based on the Practice Outlines. Be sure to have them put the extra sheets in their binders along with the appropriate Student Pages.

Follow-Up

Review the paragraphs students completed on their own. Remember that answers provided on pages 80–81 are only suggestions.

Concept to Be Taught

◉ using additional details to embellish writing

Skill to Be Learned

Students will refine their writing skills by including more descriptive and detailed information about the topic of their paragraph.

Name _____ Date _____

Using the More Detailed Outline Form for Writing

You may remember that in Section 1 you learned about the more detailed outline form. Using the simpler form, you have written paragraphs from outlines that show the main topic and the most important supporting information. With the more detailed form, you can write paragraphs that include more information— adding specific examples or more description. You won't have to leave anything out, and your paragraphs will be more interesting.

Example 1: **Imagine that you've taken notes and made an outline about pilot Amelia Earhart.**

 I. Amelia Earhart, skilled woman pilot

   A. First solo flight, 1920, age 23

   B. World altitude record for women, 14,000 feet, age 25

   C. First woman to fly solo across Atlantic

     1. 1932, age 35

     2. Newfoundland to Ireland

     3. Fifteen hours

   D. First woman to fly Honolulu to California, 1935

   E. Round world flight, 1937, with pilot Fred Noonan

     1. Lost in Pacific Ocean

     2. Believed lost near Howland Island

Take a few moments to study the outline. Notice that it uses specific dates to organize information.

What is the main topic?

_____

How many details (subtopics) support the main topic?

_____

Name _____ Date _____

Under which subtopics are there additional details?

_____

Did you choose Amelia Earhart as the main topic? Did you notice that there are five supporting details and that the subtopics with additional details are C and E?

Based on the outline, what would be a good topic sentence for a paragraph about Amelia Earhart? Write the sentence on the lines below.

_____

_____

_____

This is a sample topic sentence for a paragraph about Amelia Earhart: *Amelia Earhart, a skilled pilot, was a pioneer woman aviator.*

Now develop your own paragraph about Amelia Earhart by writing a topic sentence and supporting sentences. Be sure your topic sentence is a clear introduction of what is to come and expresses the central idea of your paragraph. Use the outline. You can use the specific dates in sequence to organize the supporting sentences. Now write your paragraph on the lines below.

_____

_____

_____

_____

_____

_____

_____

_____

_____

Name _____ Date _____

Sample Paragraph for Example Outline 1:

Amelia Earhart, a skilled pilot, was a pioneer woman aviator. In 1920, at the age of 23, Ms. Earhart made her first solo flight. Two years later she was the first woman to fly to an altitude of 14,000 feet. In 1932, at the age of 35, she became the first woman to fly solo across the Atlantic Ocean, flying from Newfoundland to Ireland in 15 hours. Three years later she flew nonstop from Honolulu to California. Her dream to be the first woman to fly around the world was shattered when she and her traveling companion, pilot Fred Noonan, were lost in the middle of the Pacific Ocean in 1937. Amelia Earhart was a brave, skilled aviator, and a model for many women of her generation.

This paragraph sequences specific dates. Dates used as signal words move the paragraph from one event to another.

Example 2: Study the following outline.

    I. Lighthouse of Alexandria, Egypt, one of the seven wonders of the ancient world
        A. Lighthouse
            1. Completed in 280 B.C.
            2. Was 410 feet high
        B. Fuel for light
            1. Burned pine branches
            2. Brought by barges
            3. Transported by mules up ramps to highest tower
            4. Hoisted by ropes and pulleys to very top
        C. Light
            1. Reflected off large rounded bronze sheets
            2. Reflected 30 miles
            3. Used for 14 centuries

The outline is organized with a main topic and three subtopics. The subtopics are in a certain order—lighthouse, fuel, light. Use this order when you develop your paragraph.

    Now write your paragraph on a separate sheet of paper. Start with a topic sentence. The central idea of the entire outline is expressed in the main topic (*Lighthouse of Alexandria, Egypt, one of the seven wonders of the ancient world*), which you can use to form a topic sentence. Don't forget to end your paragraph with a clincher. After you've written your paragraph, compare it to the one on the next page.

Name _____ Date _____

Sample Paragraph for Example Outline 2:

One of the seven wonders of the ancient world was the Lighthouse of Alexandria in Egypt. The lamp was first lighted in 280 B.C. and burned for 14 centuries. Its light was fueled by pine branches brought to the lighthouse island on barges. Mules then transported the branches up the ramps to the highest tower. Next, ropes and pulleys were used to hoist the branches 410 feet to the very top. The light of the flames reflected off the rounded bronze sheets that could be seen as far as 30 miles out to sea, providing safe passage for ships approaching the harbor. The Lighthouse of Alexandria was built to stand forever.

Was your paragraph similar to the one above? More important, did you include in your paragraph all the details given in the outline? Two signal words, *then* and *next* show a time sequence.

In the paragraph above which sentence is the topic sentence? Which sentence is the clincher? The topic sentence is: *One of the seven wonders of the ancient world was the Lighthouse of Alexandria in Egypt.* The clincher is: *The Lighthouse of Alexandria was built to stand forever.*

Name _____ Date _____

Practice Outlines

1. **Read the following outline and study the information about Arctic polar bears.**

> **I.** Arctic polar bears, large and formidable hunters
>
>   **A.** Description
>
>   **1.** Largest of all bears
>
>   **2.** Huge hairy paws
>
>   **3.** Long sharp claws
>
>   **4.** Large powerful canine teeth
>
>   **5.** Seven-foot body
>
>   **6.** Thick white hair
>
>   **B.** Hunting techniques
>
>   **1.** Sneaks up on seal's hole
>
>   **2.** Waits patiently
>
>   **3.** Attacks prey
>
>   **4.** Drags prey
>
>   **5.** Consumes prey

Using the main topic as a guide, study the entire outline and find the central idea. The outline shows us that the Arctic polar bear is a large and formidable hunter. This might be your topic sentence, or try making up one of your own.

If the Arctic polar bear is a formidable hunter, then it must have an unusually strong body. Therefore, the bear's physical makeup contributes to its success as a hunter. So the outline's subtopics, A (*Description*) and B (*Hunting techniques*), can be combined to make one paragraph.

Now, write your paragraph on a separate sheet of paper, starting with a topic sentence.

Paragraph Writing Made Easy! Scholastic Professional Books

LESSON 9: Using the More Detailed Outline Form for Writing

Name _____ Date _____

2. Here's another outline to change into a paragraph.

I. Chipmunks—members of the rodent family

   A. Appearance

      1. Small mammal—five to six inches long, four-inch bushy tail

      2. Color—reddish brown, stripes on back and side

      3. Cheek pouches to carry food

   B. Food—berries, seeds, nuts, insects

   C. Habitat—hides in woods

   D. Hibernation—winter

   E. Reproduction—two litters yearly, three to five young in litter

   F. Habits

      1. Sit upright often

      2. Raise tail straight up, make chirping noises when agitated

      3. Scurry busily

Now use a separate sheet of paper to write a topic sentence. Then add supporting sentences. Use signal words if necessary. Finally, add a clincher.

3. Read the following outline and study the information about Hank Greenberg.

I. Hank Greenberg and the baseball pennant race

   A. Cause

      1. Detroit Tigers in race for American League pennant, 1934

      2. Greenberg batting .336 in cleanup position

      3. Greenberg, not to offend Jewish parents, refused to play on Jewish holiday Yom Kippur

   B. Effect

      1. Detroit Tigers lost vital game

      2. Greenberg respected by many teammates

      3. Edgar Guest wrote poem:

> *We shall miss him on the infield*
> *And shall miss him at the bat*
> *But he's true to his religion*
> *And I honor him for that!*

Now use a separate sheet of paper to write a topic sentence and add supporting sentences. Using the information in sequence will help you organize the sentences. Use signal words. Finally, add a clincher or use the poem as a conclusion.

Name _____ Date _____

4. **Read and study the following outline presenting information about one boy who made a difference. Then use the information to write a paragraph on a separate piece of paper that includes a topic sentence and supporting sentences. Use signal words where appropriate to create transitions.**

    I. Joel, age 15, wanted something changed

        A. 1990—watched TV program

            1. Tuna fishing boats trap dolphins in tuna nets

            2. Since 1960, 10 million dolphins killed in tuna nets

        B. Joel—help from science teacher and students

            1. Discover large U.S. canning corporation owns biggest tuna wholesaler

            2. Decide to write postcards to three company executives at their homes

            3. Each student mailed six cards daily

        C. Results

            1. Executives agree to buy tuna only from fishermen who use special nets to protect dolphins

            2. Other wholesalers also agree

5. **Read and study the following outline about different kinds of African mammals. Notice that the mammals are being compared. Write your paragraph on a separate sheet of paper.**

    I. Two possible categories of African mammals: the herbivore and the carnivore

        A. Herbivore, plant-eating

            1. Kinds: elephants, giraffes, zebras, wildebeests, gazelles, and antelopes

            2. Food: plants, roots, leaves, grasses, seeds, overripe fruit

            3. Habits: travel in herds for protection, always alert to danger

        B. Carnivore, flesh-eating

            1. Kinds: lions, cheetahs, leopards, hyenas, jackals, wild dogs

            2. Food: gazelles, zebras, jackals, lion cubs, snakes, birds, domestic dogs, small prey of all kinds, porcupines

            3. Habits: live in family groups, unafraid of other animals

Name _____ Date _____

6. **Study the following outline and determine what is being contrasted. Signal words will help you organize your paragraph. Write your paragraph on a separate sheet of paper.**

    I. Misunderstandings between English and North American native peoples, starting seventeenth century

        A. English settlers

            1. Given rights to use land through treaties

            2. Cleared land

            3. Built houses and barns

            4. Felt owned land

        B. Native peoples

            1. Understood settlers would share land

            2. Believed land sacred

            3. Felt land could not be bought and sold

            4. Saw treaties broken

7. **Here is another outline to be changed into paragraph form. Write your paragraph on a separate sheet of paper.**

    I. Qualifications of Jackie Robinson, first African American major league baseball player, spring 1947

        A. Skilled ballplayer

            1. Excellent hitter

            2. Fast runner

            3. Talented second baseman

        B. Courageous man

            1. Agreed to ignore abuses for three years

                a. Ignored by teammates

                b. Taunted by fans

                c. Goaded by white press

            2. Agreed to concentrate on playing ball

Answer Suggestions

When students write their own outlines and paragraphs, their answers may differ from those given here and still be correct. Accept all reasonable responses.

SECTION 1: Understanding Paragraphs

LESSON 1: Paragraph Construction

PARAGRAPH 1 (Page 10) **Key word:** *nurses.* It is repeated four times. **Topic sentence:** *During the Vietnam War about 55,000 nurses cared for 300,000 wounded soldiers.*

PARAGRAPH 2 (Page 10) **Key word:** *course.* It is repeated seven times. **Topic sentence:** *The number of courses served in a railroad dining car in the 1920s made dinner a memorable event.*

PARAGRAPH 3 (Page 11) **Key word:** *palindrome.* It is used four times. **Topic sentence:** *A palindrome is a word or a sentence that is spelled the same backward as forward.*

PARAGRAPH 4 (Page 11) **Key words:** *Jackie Robinson, he.* They are repeated seven times. **Topic sentence:** *Jackie Robinson was one of the cleverest base runners in modern baseball.*

PARAGRAPH 5 (Page 11) **Key words:** *Georgia O'Keefe, she.* **Topic sentence:** *From the time the artist Georgia O'Keeffe was young, she was interested in painting a part of a whole scene.*

PARAGRAPH 6 (Page 12) **Key word:** *Claudette.* It is repeated seven times. **Topic sentence:** *In 1955 Claudette Colvin, a 15-year-old African-American girl, stood up for her rights.*

LESSON 2: Taking Notes in Outline Form

PARAGRAPH 1 (Page 18) **Key words:** humpback whales. **Topic sentence:** *Humpback whales are among the magnificent giants of the sea.*

Main topic:	**I.** Humpback whales
Six details:	**A.** Mammals
	B. Length, 45 feet
	C. Tail flukes, 12 feet wide
	D. Throat, 30 expanding grooves
	E. Blowholes, breathing
	F. Leap, high in air

PARAGRAPH 2 (Page 18) **Key word:** walls. **Topic sentence:** *Walls and fences are often built to keep people out or to keep people in.*

Main topic:	**I.** Walls keep people in and out
Three details:	**A.** Berlin Wall—East Germans in
	B. Prison walls—inmates in
	C. The Great Wall of China —invaders out

PARAGRAPH 3 (Page 19) **Key words:** chickadees, birds. **Topic sentence:** *The behavior of chickadees at a feeding station is always interesting to watch.*

I. Behavior of chickadees at feeders
  A. Feed one at a time
  B. Feed according to dominance
  C. Take one seed at a time
  D. Can feed upside down

PARAGRAPH 4 (Page 19) **Key word:** Heracles. **Topic sentence:** *Heracles, a very popular Greek hero, accomplished incredible deeds of strength and bravery.*

    I. Heracles accomplished strong and brave deeds
        A. Destroyed Nemean lion
        B. Killed flesh-eating cranes
        C. Captured three-headed dog, Cerberus

LESSON 3: Outlines and Parallel Construction

PARAGRAPH 1 (Page 22) **Topic sentence:** *The great left-handed pitcher Steve Carlton felt that in order to pitch well he needed to eliminate all distractions.*

    I. Steve Carlton, pitcher, eliminates distractions
        A. Stopped talking to reporters
        B. Stopped reading newspapers
        C. Stopped watching television

PARAGRAPH 2 (Page 22) **Topic sentence:** *On a small island in New York Harbor stands the Statue of Liberty.*

    I. Statue of Liberty
        A. Gift from French government
        B. Height—305 feet
        C. Torch of freedom, right hand
        D. Tablet dated July 4, 1776, left hand
        E. Crown with seven spikes for seven continents

LESSON 4: Signal Words

PARAGRAPH 1 (Page 27) **Topic Sentence:** *A good baseball catcher must develop particular skills.*
Signal words: *For example, furthermore, in addition, also*

    I. Baseball catcher's skills
        A. Catch difficult pitches
        B. Throw to catch stealing base runner
        C. Tag out runner coming home
        D. Know batter's weaknesses

PARAGRAPH 2 (Page 28) **Topic sentence:** *In 1980 Maya Ying Lin, a Chinese American, was chosen from among 1,400 artists to design the Vietnam Veterans Memorial in Washington, D.C.* **Signal words:** *when, at first, however, as a result*

    I. Maya Lin won Vietnam Veterans Memorial competition, 1980
        A. Studied architecture at Yale
        B. Designed 500-foot granite wall
        C. Designed names of 58,000 war dead
        D. Concept criticized by many at first
        E. Later earned respect of Veterans and public
        F. Visited by over one million people each year

PRACTICE PARAGRAPH 3 (Page 29) **Topic sentence:** *In 1969 a professional baseball player challenged a rule called the reserve clause, which allowed baseball owners to buy or sell players without their consent.*
Signal words: *during, now, however, eventually, although*

    I. Curt Flood, professional baseball player, challenged reserve clause
        A. Flood, Cardinals center fielder, sold to Phillies, 1969
        B. Refused to be sold, not piece of property
        C. Called reserve clause illegal, immoral
        D. Took case to court
        E. Flood lost case
        F. At end of 1970s, reserve clause terminated.

ANSWER SUGGESTIONS

LESSON 5: Types of Paragraphs

ENUMERATIVE PARAGRAPH 1 (Page 32) **Topic sentence:** *Many different kinds of timepieces have been developed over the centuries.* **Signal words:** *for example, another, examples, further examples*

    I. Different kinds of timepieces
- **A.** Sundial—Egypt—uses sun
- **B.** Grandfather clock—uses weights
- **C.** Wristwatch—uses springs
- **D.** Digital clock—uses batteries
- **E.** Possible future clocks—using nuclear energy

ENUMERATIVE PARAGRAPH 2 (Page 32) **Topic sentence:** *What qualities do you think make a great leader?* **Signal words:** *for instance, also, most important, furthermore*

    I. Examples of leadership qualities
- **A.** Solve problems
- **B.** Work with competent people
- **C.** Have a vision of future
- **D.** Persuade others to see vision
- **E.** Inspire others to follow

SEQUENCE PARAGRAPH—SAMPLE (Page 33) **Topic sentence:** *As you can see, a batter goes through several steps in preparation for coming to bat.* **Signal words:** *first, then, next, finally*

    I. Preparing to bat
- **A.** Selects favorite bat
- **B.** Moves to batter's circle
- **C.** Swings bat with weight or uses two bats
- **D.** Kneels in circle, watches pitcher
- **E.** Positions himself in batter's box
- **F.** Faces pitcher

SEQUENCE PARAGRAPH 1 (Page 34) **Topic sentence:** *The lobster industry in Maine has changed dramatically over the past hundred years.* **Signal words:** *in the old days, later on, now*

    I. Order of events in the lobster industry
- **A.** Old days, lobstering from small rowboat close to shore
- **B.** Later, lobstering by sail, farther out
- **C.** Now, lobstering with gasoline engine, large area covered

SEQUENCE PARAGRAPH 2 (Page 34) **Topic sentence:** *Justice Thurgood Marshall was an outstanding lawyer and a crusader for racial justice.* **Signal words:** *1933, then, after, soon, eventually, 1967, 1993*

    I. Justice Thurgood Marshall, outstanding lawyer, crusader for racial justice
- **A.** Graduated from Howard University's all-black law school
- **B.** Worked to fight segregation at all-white law schools
- **C.** Won case to end segregation at University of Maryland's law school
- **D.** Worked for admission of blacks to all-white public schools
- **E.** Won case in Supreme Court that ended public school segregation
- **F.** Appointed to Supreme Court, 1967
- **G.** Died in 1993

CAUSE-EFFECT PARAGRAPH—SAMPLE (Page 35) **Topic sentence:** *In 1988, a destructive earthquake hit San Francisco.*

    I. In 1988, a destructive earthquake hit San Francisco.
- **A.** Buildings rocked and collapsed
- **B.** Gas main ruptured causing fires
- **C.** Telephone and electric service was cut off
- **D.** Road and highways buckled, killing many people

ANSWER SUGGESTIONS

CAUSE-EFFECT PARAGRAPH 1 (Page 36) **Topic sentence:** *Many kinds of birds are endangered today because of irresponsible human behavior.* **Signal words:** *effect, resulted in*

    I. Birds endangered because of irresponsible human behavior
        A. Conversion of wetlands to agricultural lands—destroys habitats
        B. Oil and chemical spills—kill birds
        C. Tree cutting—disturbs breeding grounds

CAUSE-EFFECT PARAGRAPH 2 (Page 36) **Topic sentence:** *The sinking of the unsinkable* Titanic *was one of the great sea disasters.* **Signal words:** *April 1912, April 14, later, as a result*

    I. Sinking of *Titanic* great sea disaster, human negligence
        A. Maiden voyage, England to New York
        B. Icebergs sighted in North Atlantic
        C. Collision 11:40 P.M., April 14, 1912
        D. 300-foot gash in bow of ship
        E. Lifeboats saved only half the passengers and crew
        F. *Titanic* sank
        G. 1,500 people drowned

COMPARE/CONTRAST PARAGRAPH 1 (Page 39) **Topic sentence:** *People everywhere—regardless of culture, religion, race, sex, or age—possess many of the same needs.* **Signal words:** *first, in addition, furthermore*

    I. All people everywhere have the same needs.
        A. Music—to survive and flourish
        B. Neighbors—to help each other in times of trouble
        C. Freedom—to define ourselves

COMPARE/CONTRAST PARAGRAPH 2 (Page 39) **Topic sentence:** *The most difficult position on a baseball team is that of catcher, and most of us loyal fans assume that the position requires a strong if not burly male.* **Signal words:** *for example, however, during*

    I. Does difficult catcher position require strong male?
        A. Strong male catchers: Berra, Fisk, Campanella, Bench
        B. Skilled female catchers: Dorothy "Dottie" Green, Mary Rountree

DESCRIPTIVE PARAGRAPH—SAMPLE (Page 40)

    I. Statue of Liberty located in New York Harbor
        A. Gift from French government
        B. 305 feet tall
        C. Holds torch of freedom in right hand
        D. Hold tablet dated July 4, 1776, in left hand
        E. Wears crown with seven spikes representing seven continents

DESCRIPTIVE PARAGRAPH 1 (Page 41) **Topic sentence:** *Scientists found a baby dinosaur nest in Montana in the 1980s.*

    I. Baby dinosaur nest found in Montana in 1980s
        A. Nest—three feet deep, six feet wide
        B. Baby dinosaur skeletons found
        C. Babies—three feet long, two months old
        D. Babies related to duck-billed dinosaur
        E. Babies lived 60 million years ago

DESCRIPTIVE PARAGRAPH 2 (Page 41) **Topic sentence:** *The dolphin belongs to a group of mammals called cetaceans.*

    I. Dolphin—a mammal
        A. Live birth, breathe air, warm blood
        B. Grow to 12 feet, weigh over 400 lbs.
        C. Have no fur on hind legs
        D. Dive 70 feet deep, leap 30 feet high
        E. Submerge for 15 minutes
        F. Hear well, no sense of smell
        G. Train to perform

LESSON 6: More Detailed Outline Form

PARAGRAPH 1 (Page 47) **Topic sentence:** *When our founding fathers wrote the Bill of Rights, they wrote about rights and responsibilities.* **Signal words:** *first, second*

    I. Rights and responsibilities of Bill of Rights
        A. Rights of citizens
            1. Freedom of speech
            2. Freedom to practice religion
            3. Freedom to buy property
            4. Freedom to have trial by jury
            5. Freedom to vote
        B. Responsibilities of citizens
            1. Vote
            2. Serve on juries
            3. Write to president and representatives in Congress
            4. Protest injustices
            5. Improve life in communities

PARAGRAPH 2 (Page 47) **Topic sentence:** *The Wabanakis (Wah/buh/nah/keys), the native people who lived in the area now called New England, suffered greatly from diseases brought by European settlers.* **Signal words:** *for example, furthermore, in addition, although*

    I. Wabanakis suffered from diseases brought by European settlers
        A. Had no immunity
            1. Measles
            2. Scarlet fever
            3. Smallpox
         B. Received little help from former methods of treating disease
            1. Herbal medicines
            2. Medicine men
         C. Found it difficult to care for each other
        D. Survived to this day

PARAGRAPH 3 (Page 48) **Topic sentence:** *Since dams built across large rivers prevent fish from returning to spawning grounds upstream, two kinds of apparatus have been developed to help the fish.*

    I. Apparatus to help fish spawn upstream
        A. Fish ladder
            1. Series of platforms
                a. Platform four to five feet high
                b. Water flows, creating waterfalls
            2. Fish jump up against waterfall to top

B. Fish lift

    1. Bargelike container at foot of dam

        a. Fish swim in

        b. Fish lifted to top

    2. Fish transported in trucks to spawning grounds

PARAGRAPH 4 (Page 49) **Topic sentence:** *Biologist Rachel Carson was a woman of great vision and courage.*

I. Rachel Carson, biologist, woman of vision and courage

    A. Education and Jobs

        1. Grade-school student—examined sea and land animals

        2. Graduate student

            a. Studied biology—Marine Biological Lab, Woods Hole

            b. Studied genetics—Johns Hopkins University

        3. Jobs

            a. Worked for U.S. Bureau of Fisheries

            b. Worked for Fish and Wildlife Service

        4. Independent research

            a. Studied synthetic insecticides

            b. Studied effect on land, water, plants, and animals

    B. Major publication

        1. *Silent Spring* exposed use and danger of deadly chemicals

    C. Federal government responds

        1. Founded Environmental Protection Agency

        2. Banned most dangerous insecticides

PARAGRAPH 5 (Page 50) **Topic sentence:** *The experience of two different cultures in an earlier period might offer helpful models for alleviating some of the problems of families today.*

I. Family experience of two cultures

    A. Iroquois family, seventeenth century

        1. Included mother father, children, grandparents, aunts, uncles, cousins

        2. Lived together in a single space

        3. Ate, worked, played together

        4. Shared responsibilities

        5. Contributed to good of community

    B. Jewish family in Palestine, mid-nineteenth century

        1. Adults

            a. Worked in fields

            b. Cared for children

            c. Taught children

        2. Children

            a. Had daily classes

            b. Had daily jobs

            c. Shared responsibilities

            d. Contributed to good of community

SECTION 2: Writing Paragraphs

The paragraphs shown in this section represent examples of paragraphs written from the outlines provided on the Student Pages. Your students' paragraphs will not be written exactly like these. Their paragraphs will include the relevant information in the outline and, in addition, information they have added to the outline through class discussion, individual conversations, or by using reference books.

LESSON 7: Using Notes to Write Paragraphs

OUTLINE 1 (Page 55)
Main topic: humpback whales
Number of supporting details: 6

LESSON 8: Using Signal Words

OUTLINE 1 (Page 62)

Long ago, the Ojibway people, living on land that is now Minnesota, respected the land and all living things. They did not own land but shared it with one another and with the animals. The Ojibway considered trees a sacred gift that provided shelter for people and animals. They cut only enough wood, roots, and bark to build their lodges. Furthermore, they cherished life and killed only those animals needed for food and clothing. The Ojibway people were careful to waste nothing and to share all they had.

OUTLINE 2 (Page 63)

During World War II young Anne Frank, a Jew, had to hide in order to escape the persecution of the Nazis. For two years Anne and her family lived in a secret apartment in the attic area of Mr. Frank's business building in Amsterdam. Four of Mr. Frank's former employees became the Franks' lifeline to survival. The radio, turned on when the warehouse workers had left, gave them news and eventual hope for survival. The family celebrated all special days together. Jewish holidays and birthdays were particularly important for their morale. Furthermore, they all continued to study and learn. In August of 1944 the secret attic area was discovered. Anne was sent to a concentration camp, where she died of typhus in April 1945. All who kept the secret of the apartment for two years were courageous.

OUTLINE 3 (Page 64)

The marathon race, starting with one runner in 490 B.C., has developed into a race of thousands of runners. In the beginning, one Greek soldier ran from the battlefield of Marathon to Athens, a distance of 22 miles, to tell of the victory of the Greeks over the Persians. In 1896 Greece held the first modern marathon, duplicating the original run. In 1897 Boston held its first marathon. The distance of that race increased to 25 miles. In 1908 it increased to 26 miles for the Olympic Games in England. By 1970, New York City held its own marathon race with 127 runners. Today many thousands of runners race in marathon races in cities all over the world.

LESSON 9: Using the More Detailed Outline Form for Writing

OUTLINE 1 (Page 70)

The Arctic polar bear is a large and formidable hunter. This enormous animal has huge hairy paws, long sharp claws, and powerful canine teeth. Its huge seven-foot body is covered with thick white hair. When the Arctic polar bear hunts a seal, first it silently pads up to the seal hole in the ice, waiting patiently for the seal to stick its head out of the water. Then, with a powerful blow of its huge paw, the bear kills its prey, drags it out of the hole, and tears its flesh with its powerful teeth. The polar bear is the largest of all bears.

OUTLINE 2 (Page 71)

Chipmunks are among the most attractive and appealing members of the rodent family. A chipmunk is a small mammal, five to six inches long with a four-inch bushy tail. It is reddish brown with stripes on its backs and sides. Chipmunks eat berries, seeds, nuts, and insects, and often carry food in their cheek pouches. In the fall they burrow into holes where they store some of their food. In the winter chipmunks hibernate, and in the spring they leave their holes and look for food and mates. Chipmunks are fun to watch as they scurry about collecting food. They often sit upright, surveying the area. However, when they are agitated, their tail goes straight up and they repeatedly makes chirping noises. Chipmunks are wonderful to watch.

OUTLINE 3 (Page 71)

Hank Greenberg decided it was more important to stand up for his beliefs than to play a decisive baseball game. In 1934 the Detroit Tigers were in a race for the American League pennant, and